20 Ways to Cook
MACKEREL

Gail Duff

Thomas Harmsworth Publishing Company

First Published 1994 by
Thomas Harmsworth Publishing
Company
Old Rectory Offices
Stoke Abbott
Beaminster
Dorset DT8 3JT

British Library Cataloguing-in-Publication
Data. A catalogue record for this book is
available from the British Library.

ISSN 1355-4050
ISBN 0 948807 23 7

Printed and bound in Great Britain by
BPC Paulton Books Ltd.

CONTENTS

INTRODUCTION

Mackerel is cheap, versatile and highly nutritious. The fish are caught off the North Atlantic coasts of the United States and Europe and are available for most of the year. Besides being a part of commercial catches, mackerel are frequently caught by amateur fishermen out on one-day fishing trips and, as such, are the fish that many fishermen's wives have to deal with most frequently. With the recipes that follow, a glut of mackerel can be put to huge advantage.

The whole fish are attractive in appearance, almost black along the top, with lights of greeny-blue, this dark patch then becoming curving lines which stand out against the silver sides. Although a mackerel does have scales, they are small and flat and not at all apparent. They do not have to be removed, making the fish easy to prepare for cooking.

Mackerel are called 'oily fish.' That is to say, the natural fish oils are distributed throughout the flesh instead of being confined to the liver, as in white fish such as cod. This makes the flesh firm, on the dark side, and very rich to eat. Its main vitamins are A and D and the oil contained in it is rich in polyunsaturated fats: those which are said to lower cholesterol levels.

Being a fairly small fish, mackerel can be cooked whole or filleted. They can be grilled, fried, baked or poached, served hot or cold, and with a great variety of accompaniments or flavourings. Preparing a mackerel for cooking is neither difficult nor time consuming and cooking times are usually short and methods uncomplicated.

If you have never considered mackerel before, now is the time to try it and here are recipes to enable you to make the most of that frequent glut.

AVAILABILITY

Fresh mackerel is generally available throughout the year, although the fish themselves may vary in size according to the season. Mackerel can be bought from fishmongers and from the fish counter in supermarkets. It is frequently to be found on sale at coastal resorts, usually fresh from the sea that day. It is not usually sold frozen.

Mackerel is usually sold whole. The fish are normally cleaned and, if this is not the case, most fishmongers will clean fish on request. Some supermarkets sell prepacked mackerel, cleaned and with heads and tails removed. You may also find mackerel fillets sold in this way.

SIZES AND SERVINGS

Mackerel vary considerably in size, often according to the time of year. Small whole mackerel weigh 6 - 8 oz (175 - 225 g) before cleaning; medium sized 8 - 12 oz (225 - 350 g); and large mackerel above 12 oz (350 g).

One small to medium sized mackerel will serve one person. When only large mackerel are available, always choose a recipe in which the fish are filleted and allow one fillet per person.

STORING

Mackerel are best eaten on the day of purchase, but you can keep them for 24 hours in the refrigerator, provided that they are cleaned before storing.

Mackerel can be frozen uncooked, either whole or filleted. Whole mackerel should be cleaned and individually wrapped. Use cling-film for each separate fish and then store the fish together in a sealed polythene bag. Fillets should be individually wrapped in clingfilm and then stored together in a sealed polythene bag.

Store mackerel in the freezer for up to one month. Thaw it in the refrigerator before cooking.

PREPARATION (FRESH MACKEREL)

Cleaning. If you have a whole fresh mackerel that you are going to fillet and eat on the day of purchase, there is no need to individually clean each fish. Mackerel that are to be stored in the refrigerator or freezer should be cleaned beforehand. All mackerel should be cleaned if they are going to be cooked whole.

To clean a mackerel, take a sharp knife and slit the fish along the belly from just in front of the side fins to the first main belly fin which marks the end of the body cavity. The guts of the fish can easily be taken out of the body cavity through this slit. You may need to cut them just under the head.

When the fish are cleaned, rinse them under cold, running water and dry them with kitchen paper.

Lay the fish once more on the chopping board and open them up. You will see a line of dark blood underneath a thin skin covering running all the way down the central bone. This is called the blood line. Scrape it away with the tip of a sharp knife.

There is also a thin, dark skin on the side of the fillet. Scrape this away as well. Wash and dry the fish again.

Preparing Cleaned Fish. Check that the blood line and the dark skin have been removed.

Preparing Fish for Cooking Whole. Whole fish are often cooked with their heads on. If you find this unacceptable, cut off the head just behind the front side fin. A sharp knife will slice all the way through the flesh and the backbone.

Cut off the side fins and the back fins using a small sharp knife by holding the fin in one hand while you cut just underneath it using the other. Cut off the tiny fins which are underneath the fish, running up to the tail.

Mackerel tails are V-shaped but the inner part of the V tends to be slightly ragged. Make a good, even point by trimming the uneven parts with kitchen snippers or sharp scissors. This is called to 'Van Dyke' the tail, i.e. you are making an even point like that of a Van Dyke beard.

If you are going to grill the fish, cut three diagonal slits in the flesh, running backwards and downwards from head to tail and evenly spaced. Cut just down as far as the back bone in the thickest part and leave about ½ inch (1.3 cm) at the top and bottom of the fish. This helps the thicker parts of the fish to cook at the same rate as the thinner.

Filleting a mackerel. To fillet a mackerel, there is no need to remove the fins or to even clean the fish first. You will need a good, sharp kitchen knife. Slit through the flesh of the fish to the backbone on either side of the fish, just behind the front side fin. For the first fillet, lay the fish, belly away from you on a chopping board. At the tip of the slit that you have made behind the fin, turn the knife so that it is flat, blade towards the tail. Cut along the back line of the fish keeping the knife just above the back fins as the fish is lying down. Continue to the tail end and then ease the fillet away from the bone. Cut down the belly to separate the fillet. Turn the fish over and cut off the second fillet working once again with your knife held flat and this time from the tail towards the head.

When you have two separate fillets, remove any small bones that are still attached to the thicker end and scrape away the thin layer of black skin that is on the thinner edge.

Making one large fillet. To make one large fillet, clean the fish and cut off the head and the tail. Turn the fish belly towards you. Holding your knife flat and with your other hand pressing lightly down on the side of the fish, slit between the flesh and the backbone, separating the bone from one fillet, but stop when you are about ½ inch (1.3 cm) from the top of the fish. Open the fish out and lay it, cut side down, on the chopping board. Press down firmly with your forefinger along the line of the backbone. Turn the fish over and gently ease the backbone away from the flesh. You may have to use your knife on the thicker part. Turn the fillet, cut side down again, on the chopping board. Gently stretch up the central back bone and cut it away with kitchen snippers or sharp scissors. (If you cut it out with a knife you will end up with a hole in the fillet).

BASIC COOKING METHODS

Grilling whole. Prepare the fish as above. Brush the fish inside and out with a mixture of oil and lemon juice, or oil and vinegar, or with a marinade (see page 9). Leave the fish to stand for at least 30 minutes if you are using a marinade.

Preheat the grill to high and, if you have an open, wire rack, cover it with foil. Lay the whole fish on the hot rack and grill for about 4 minutes on each side, or until the fish are cooked through and lightly browned.

Grilling fillets. Brush the fillets with oil, or with a mixture of oil and lemon juice, or oil and vinegar. Alternatively, turn them in a marinade and leave them for at least 1 hour at room temperature.

To cook, heat the grill to high and, if you have an open, wire rack, cover it with foil. Lay the fillets, cut side up, on the hot rack or foil. Grill them for 4 - 5 minutes, without turning.

Frying whole. Prepare the fish as for grilling whole (above), with slits in the side. The heads and tails may be cut off if wished. Coat in seasoned flour and fry in oil or butter on a medium heat for about 5 minutes each side or until cooked through. Should the mackerel be on the large side and need longer cooking, lower the heat after 10 minutes and continue cooking until they are done.

Frying fillets. The fillets may be coated in seasoned flour or left plain. Heat oil or butter in a large heavy frying pan on a medium heat. Put in the fillets, cut side down first, and fry them for about 3 minutes on each side or until they are golden brown and cooked through. You will probably not fit all the fillets in the pan at any one time. If this is the case, fry as many as will fit in, put them onto a heatproof plate and keep them warm in a low oven while you fry the rest.

Stir-frying. Cut mackerel fillets into strips or small squares. Stir-fry in hot oil for about 3 minutes or until the pieces are cooked through but not soft enough to break up.

Poaching. Mackerel is best filleted before poaching. Make a poaching liquid known as a *court bouillon* by putting enough water in a wide-based pan to cover the mackerel. Add a bouquet garni, ½ teaspoon black peppercorns, one slice of onion, a small piece of carrot and a small piece of celery stick. Bring them to the boil and add a squeeze of lemon juice or 4 tablespoons of dry white wine or cider. Reduce the heat so the liquid is just trembling. Alternatively, use a good quality court bouillon or fish stock cube. Carefully ease in the fillets. Poach them for about 4 minutes or until they are cooked through but not falling apart. Lift them out with a fish slice and drain them well.

Microwaving. To cook whole mackerel, cut off the heads and tails and remove the backbones as in the method for making one large fillet (above). Fold the fillets to reshape them. Brush them with oil or a mixture of oil and lemon juice or vinegar. Lay the re-shaped fish in a microwave-proof dish and cover them. Cook on high for 3 minutes. Turn the fish over and cook on high for a further 3 minutes. Leave to stand for 5 minutes.

Brush fillets with oil or a mixture of oil and lemon juice or vinegar. Put them into a micro-wave-proof dish and cover them. Microwave on high for 3 minutes and let stand for 2 minutes.

Pressure cooking. Follow manufacturer's instructions.

HERBS TO FLAVOUR MACKEREL

Basil: Sprinkle chopped over fillets before grilling or baking. Put sprigs inside whole fish.

Bay: Put into the dish when baking mackerel or into the stock when poaching.

Chervil: Use whole sprigs or leaves as a garnish for any mackerel dish. Put whole sprigs or leaves inside whole fish before cooking or alongside fillets when baking. Use chopped as a substitute for chopped parsley.

Chives: Chop and sprinkle over fillets before grilling or baking.

Coriander: Use coriander leaves as a garnish and put chopped fresh coriander into mackerel salads and into stir-fried dishes. Add a little ground coriander to marinades, particularly when other curry spices such as cumin are being used.

Dill: Scatter chopped fresh dill over fillets before grilling or baking. Lay whole sprigs inside whole fish or in the dish alongside fillets when baking. Use in salads and stir-fried dishes.

Fennel: Use chopped in salads, stir-fried dishes and patés. Use leaves for garnish. Scatter chopped leaves over fillets before grilling or use in marinades. Put sprigs inside whole fish before cooking.

Mint: Put sprigs inside whole fish before grilling or baking to give clean taste.

Parsley: Use as a garnish and in salads, scattered over fillets or into whole fish before grilling or baking. Add to patés and sauces. Put into poaching stock.

Thyme: Put sprigs into whole fish before grilling or roasting. Scatter chopped thyme over fillets before cooking. Put sprigs into poaching stock. Add to salads.

SPICES TO FLAVOUR MACKEREL

Before grilling or baking, sprinkle the fish with a little of any of the following. Add the same mixtures to oil for basting or to marinades.

Ground cardamom, alone or mixed in equal parts with cumin

or cayenne pepper or chili powder

or ground cinnamon

or mustard powder

or freshly-grated nutmeg

or ground mace

or paprika, alone or mixed with cayenne pepper or chili powder

MARINADES FOR MACKEREL

A basic marinade for 4 small-medium mackerel: 4 tablespoons olive or sunflower oil, 2 tablespoons cider vinegar, or white wine vinegar, or lemon juice or orange juice (freshly squeezed), grated rind of orange or lemon according to which fruit used. A small, chopped onion may also be added.

When making a marinade, use any of the herbs or spices listed above but make sure the flavours of the ingredients blend together.

Examples:

4 tablespoons oil, 2 tablespoons cider vinegar, ½ teaspoon ground cinnamon or nutmeg;

or 4 tablespoons oil, 2 tablespoons white wine vinegar, 2 tablespoons chopped fennel;

or 4 tablespoons oil, 2 tablespoons lemon juice, 1 teaspoon ground coriander, 1 teaspoon cumin seeds;

or 4 tablespoons oil, 2 tablespoons orange juice, 1 tablespoon tomato purée, 1 small onion, 2 tablespoons chopped parsley.

SAUCES FOR MACKEREL

Horseradish Sauce
4 tablespoons preserved grated horseradish
½ teaspoon mustard powder
2 teaspoons white wine vinegar
4 tablespoons soured cream

Mix all the ingredients together.

Butter Sauce
2 egg yolks
2 tablespoons white wine or cider vinegar
4 oz (125 g) unsalted butter, in small pieces
herbs to taste (parsley, chervil, fennel are the best)

Put the egg yolks into a bowl and stand the bowl in a saucepan of water. Set the saucepan on a low heat. Beat the egg yolks with a wooden spoon and gradually beat in the vinegar. Keep stirring on the heat until the mixture thickens and coats the back of a wooden spoon. Put in the butter and stir until it has melted and the sauce is thick. Take the bowl from the heat and stir in the herbs. Serve warm so the butter remains melted.

SMOKED MACKEREL

There are two methods of smoking: hot smoking and cold smoking, sometimes called kippering.

For *hot smoking,* fish fillets are smoked over a relatively high temperature, a process which cooks, colours and flavours. For cold smoking, the temperature is reduced. The fish fillets are coloured and flavoured by the process but not cooked through.

A large proportion of the smoked mackerel fillets available in the shops have been hot smoked. This means they are cooked through and ready to eat as they are. Smoked mackerel fillets vary a little in size but, on average, one fillet weighs 4 oz (125 g).

Hot smoked mackerel fillets may be served with a salad with no preparation at all. Should you wish to skin them, the skin will pull off easily in one piece. To flake smoked mackerel, gently pull the sections of the fillet apart, either with a knife and fork or with your fingers. Smoked mackerel fillets can be heated quickly under a high grill, or they can be made into part of a stir-fried dish, particularly one which contains rice.

Cold smoked mackerel, or kippered mackerel, can be bought in some fishmongers and supermarkets. The fillets are not cooked and are best poached, grilled or fried. Should kippered mackerel not be available for a recipe, use kipper fillets instead.

GLOSSARY

Allspice: Allspice consists of small, dark brown berries which in appearance are rather like large peppercorns. Another name for it is Jamaican pepper. In flavour, allspice is quite different to pepper. There is no trace of hotness and the flavour it gives to both savoury and sweet dishes is both delicate and sweet.

Capers: Capers are small, pungent-flavoured green buds. They are sold in small jars, pickled in vinegar and can be bought from most supermarkets, grocers shops and delicatessens.

Cayenne pepper: Cayenne pepper is a hot, red pepper with a sharp, clean flavour. It is produced by grinding several hot varieties of capsicum (a 'family' which includes sweet red and green peppers).

Chili powder: Chili powder is a mixture of cayenne pepper, paprika, cumin, cloves, marjoram and garlic, although the cayenne is the dominant flavour.

Coriander: Coriander is a herb. The leaves are used fresh and the seeds dried. The leaves are similar in appearance to flat parsley and their flavour is spicy and pungent. Coriander seeds have a sweet, spicy flavour. They are frequently used in curries, used either ground or coarsely crushed.

Dijon mustard: Dijon mustard is a smooth, spicy, very mild mustard, made originally around

Dijon in France. If it is not available use any type of smooth French mustard, or even a smooth German mustard.

Dill: Dill is a herb which has feathery shaped, fresh-tasting leaves. It is often used to give flavour to cucumber dishes. Dried dill is known as dill weed to distinguish it from the dill seeds which are also used in cooking.

Horseradish: Horseradish is the root of a plant which grows both wild and cultivated in Europe and North America. It can be bought grated and preserved in vinegar and this is the form in which it is used in the recipes in this book. If it is unavailable in this form, you can buy dried horseradish. This needs to be soaked until it is soft in a mild vinegar such as a white wine or a cider vinegar and stored in air-tight jars. Should you ever buy horseradish root, scrub the roots well and grate them, preferably in the closed top of a food processor. Pack the grated root into jars and cover it with vinegar. If none of these types of horseradish is available you can get away with using a little prepared horseradish sauce, but make sure that the variety that you choose is not too sweet.

Lettuce, battavia, escarole, frisée: These are all types of lettuce with curled or cut leaves. They have a light, crisp flavour and make ideal garnishes as well as salads.

Mace: Mace is the outer covering of the nutmeg as it grows on the tree. Once dried it becomes bright yellow and it can be bought ground in the form of a bright ochre-coloured powder. Its flavour is similar to that of nutmeg but slightly more delicate. If mace is unavailable, you may use nutmeg instead.

Muscovado sugar: Muscovado sugar is unre-
fined brown sugar which is produced from
sugar cane in its country of origin instead of
from sugar beet. Both dark and light varieties
are produced and any will be suitable for the
recipes in this book. Ordinary sugar may be
used if it is not available.

Paprika: Paprika is a dark coloured, orange-red
spice with a mild, aromatic, bitter-sweet flavour. It is produced by drying and grinding a
mild species of capsicum.

Yeast: Yeast is the micro-organism which makes
bread rise. It can be bought fresh or dried.
Fresh yeast is usually obtainable from bakers
and health shops and dried from any grocer
or supermarket. Easy-bake yeast is also available. For the amounts of this needed, follow
the instructions on the packet as to the amount
of flour specified in any particular recipe.

TABLE OF OVEN TEMPERATURES

	Fahrenheit (F)	Celsius (C)	Gas mark
	150	70	
	175	80	
	200	100	
Very cool	225	110	¼
	250	120	½
	275	140	1
Cool	300	150	2
Warm	325	160	3
Moderate/ Medium	350	180	4

Fairly Hot	375	190	5
	400	200	6
Hot	425	220	7
	450	230	8
Very hot	475	240	9
	500	260	9

IMPERIAL/METRIC CONVERSIONS

Dry weight		Liquid measure	
ounces	grams	fluid ounces	millilitres
1	25	1	25
2	50	2	50
3	75	3	75-90
4 (¼ lb)	125	4	125
5	150	5 (¼ pint)	150
6	175	6	175
7	200	7	200
8 (½ lb)	225	8	225
9	250	9	250
10	275	10 (½ pint)	275
11	300	11	300
12 (¾ lb)	350	12	350
13	375	13	375
14	400	14	400
15	425	15 (¾pint)	425
16 (1 lb)	450	16	450
17	475	17	475
18	500	18	500
2¼ lb	1000 (1 kilo)	20 (1 pint)	550
		1¾ pints	1000 (1 litre)

MACKEREL WITH TOMATO AND LEMON SAUCE

Serves: 4
Type of dish: Cold first course
Suitable for main course: yes, see below
1st preparation time: 30 minutes
Cooking time: 20 minutes
Waiting time: 1 - 1½ hours for cooling
2nd preparation time: 30 minutes
Preparation start: 3 hours before serving
Suitable for dinner parties: yes
Special equipment: ovenproof dish; sieve
Suitable for microwave cooking: yes
Suitable for pressure cooking: yes
Suitable for freezing: yes
Calorie content: medium
Carbohydrate content: low
Fibre content: low
Protein content: high
Fat content: medium

2 small mackerel
oil for greasing
1 tablespoon chopped lemon thyme, or common thyme or 1 teaspoon dried thyme
1 tablespoon chopped parsley
grated rind and juice 1 lemon
1 small onion, thinly sliced
8 oz (225 g) tomatoes
1 teaspoon paprika
2 teaspoons dark muscovado sugar
lettuce or other salad leaves for serving
4 thin lemon slices or 4 parsley sprigs for garnish

Heat the oven to 350F/180C/gas 4. Fillet the mackerel (page 5), cut each fillet in half crossways and lay the pieces flat in a lightly oiled, oven-proof dish. Sprinkle the herbs and lemon rind over the top and cover the fillets with onion slices. Chop the tomatoes and arrange them on top of the onions. Sprinkle in the paprika and sugar and pour in the lemon juice. Cover the dish with foil and put it into the oven for 20 minutes.

Leave the contents of the dish, still covered, until they are completely cold. With your fingers, carefully brush the pieces of onion and tomato from the mackerel, reserving them. Lay two pieces of mackerel fillet on each of four small plates. Garnish them with lettuce or other salad leaves. Rub the contents of the cooking dish through a sieve to make a smooth sauce. Spoon it over the mackerel. Garnish the mackerel with twists of lemon or with parsley sprigs.

Chef's tips:
☆ The garnish can be varied. For example, you can use sprigs of fennel instead of parsley or rings of sliced, stuffed olive or black olive halves instead of the lemon twists.

☆ Serve with hot rolls or baguettes.

☆ To serve as a main course, double all quantities. Serve on separate dinner plates and accompany the mackerel with a mixed salad plus a salad of rice, pasta or potatoes.

☆ To freeze, put the mackerel pieces, without sauce, in a single layer in a flat plastic container and cover. Freeze the sieved sauce separately. Store for up to two weeks. Thaw in the refrigerator and bring up to room temperature for serving.

GRILLED WHOLE MACKEREL

Serves: 4
Type of dish: hot main course (two)
Suitable for first course: no
Preparation time: 30 minutes
Waiting time: 1 hour for *Lemon Mackerel*
Cooking time: 10 minutes
Preparation start time: 45 minutes before serving *Mackerel with Horseradish;* 1 hour 45 minutes before serving *Lemon Mackerel*
Suitable for dinner parties: yes
Special equipment: grill
Suitable for microwave cooking: yes
Suitable for pressure cooking: no
Suitable for freezing: no
Calorie content: high
Carbohydrate content: low
Fibre content: low
Protein content: high
Fat content: high

4 small - medium sized mackerel
for Mackerel with Horseradish:
3 tablespoons preserved grated horseradish
2 teaspoons paprika
1 tablespoon tomato purée
2 tablespoons chopped parsley
4 tablespoons olive or sunflower oil
1 garlic clove, crushed
for Lemon Mackerel:
2 tablespoons chopped lemon thyme, or ordinary thyme
2 tablespoons chopped mint
1 teaspoon ground coriander
grated rind and juice 1 lemon
3 tablespoons olive or sunflower oil
freshly-ground black pepper

For both recipes, clean the mackerel and cut off the fins. The heads can be removed if wished. Van Dyke the tails (page 4). Rinse the mackerel under cold water and dry them with paper towels. Make three incisions on each side of the mackerel, running backwards and downwards from head to tail.

For the *mackerel with horseradish,* mix together 1 teaspoon of the paprika, the tomato purée and the parsley. Press the mixture into the slits in the mackerel. Mix the remaining paprika with the oil and garlic and brush the mixture over the outside and the inside of the mackerel.

For the *lemon mackerel,* mix together the thyme, mint, coriander and lemon rind plus 1 tablespoon of the oil. Mix the rest of the oil with the lemon juice and season with the pepper. Lay the mackerel on a flat dish and brush them inside and out with the lemon juice mixture. Press the herb mixture into the slits and let the mackerel stand for at least an hour at room temperature.

When you are ready to cook, preheat the grill to the highest temperature and, if you have and open, wire rack, cover it with foil. Lay the mackerel on the hot rack and grill them for about 4 minutes on each side, or until they are cooked through and the skin is lightly browned.

☆　　☆　　☆

Chef's tips:

☆ Garnish the Mackerel with Horseradish with watercress and the Lemon Mackerel with salad cress.

☆ Serve both types of mackerel with sauté potatoes, French fried potatoes, jacket potatoes or with potatoes that have been cut into rings and browned in the oven in a mixture of oil and butter.

☆ A green salad or tomato salad is the best accompaniment.

☆ For horseradish, see glossary, page 12.

Grilled Mackerel Fillets

GRILLED MACKEREL FILLETS

Serves: 4
Type of dish: hot main course (two)
Suitable for first course: yes, see below
Preparation time: 40 minutes
Waiting time: 1 hour
Cooking time: 10 minutes
Preparation start: 2 hours before serving
Suitable for dinner parties: yes
Special equipment: grill
Suitable for microwave cooking: yes
Suitable for pressure cooking: no
Suitable for freezing: no
Calorie content: high
Carbohydrate content: low
Fibre content: low
Protein content: high
Fat content: high

4 small - medium mackerel
for Mackerel with Orange and Tomato
2 medium oranges
2 tablespoons olive or sunflower oil
2 tablespoons tomato purée
I small onion, finely chopped
4 small, firm tomatoes
I tablespoon chopped parsley
for Mackerel with Apples
4 tablespoons olive or sunflower oil
2 tablespoons cider vinegar
I teaspoon ground cinnamon
freshly-ground black pepper
I medium sized cooking apple

Fillet the mackerel (page 5). For the *Mackerel with Orange and Tomato,* in a large, flat dish, mix together the grated rind and juice of one of the oranges, the oil, 1 tablespoon of the tomato purée and the onion. Turn the mackerel fillets in the mixture and leave them for 1 hour at room temperature.

Cut the peel and pith from the remaining orange and thinly slice it. Thinly slice the tomatoes. Spread a little of the tomato purée on each of the orange slices.

To cook, heat the grill to the highest temperature and, if you have an open wire rack, cover it with foil. Lay the mackerel fillets, cut side up, on the hot rack, still with the pieces of onion clinging to them. Grill them for 5 minutes, without turning.

Arrange tomato and orange slices on the

mackerel fillets and scatter a little parsley over the tomatoes. Return the mackerel to the grill for 1½ minutes, so the topping heats through.

For the *Mackerel with Apples*, in a large, flat dish, mix together the oil, vinegar, cinnamon and pepper. Turn the mackerel fillets in the mixture and leave them for 1 hour at room temperature.

When you are ready to cook, heat the grill to high and, if you have an open, wire rack, cover it with aluminium foil. Lay the mackerel fillets on the hot rack, skin side up, and grill them for 5 minutes.

Core and thinly slice the apple. Cut the slices into halves or quarters if they are large. Turn the pieces of apple in any marinade remaining in the dish and arrange them on top of the mackerel. Return the mackerel to the grill for 1 - 2 minutes, for the apple slices to heat through.

☆   ☆   ☆

Chef's tips:
☆ Garnish the mackerel with orange and tomato with parsley sprigs, and the mackerel with apple with watercress.
☆ Serve with mixed or green salads and with jacket or sauté potatoes.
☆ To serve as a first course, use small mackerel and allow one fillet per person. Keep the marinating ingredients the same. Halve the apple or orange and tomato.

MACKEREL KEBABS

Serves: 4
Type of dish: Hot main course
Suitable for first course: yes, see below
Preparation time: 1 hour
Waiting time: 2 hours
Cooking time: 15 minutes
Preparation start: 3¼ hours before serving
Suitable for dinner parties: yes
Special equipment: kebab skewers; large flat dish; grill
Suitable for microwave cooking: yes, use wooden skewers
Suitable for pressure cooking: no
Suitable for freezing: yes
Calorie content: high
Carbohydrate content: low
Fibre content: low
Protein content: high
Fat content: high

2 medium mackerel
4 oz (125 g) lean back bacon
4 oz (125 g) button mushrooms
1 medium onion
2 medium green peppers
4 bay leaves
2 tablespoons olive oil
juice 1 lemon
2 tablespoons chopped thyme
freshly-ground black pepper
for serving:
1 lettuce or a mixture of salad leaves and radishes

Fillet the mackerel (page 5) and cut the fillets into 1 inch (2.5 cm) squares. Derind the bacon and cut it into 1 inch (2.5 cm) squares. If the mushrooms are small, leave them whole. They can also be halved, or quartered, according to their size. Cut the onions into pieces about 1 inch (2.5 cm) square, separating the layers. Core and seed the peppers and cut them into square pieces the same size.

Alternate pieces of mackerel, bacon, mushroom, pepper, onion and bayleaf on each of four kebab skewers. Put the kebabs onto a large, flat dish.

Beat together the oil and lemon juice and pour it over the kebabs. Strew the kebabs with thyme and grind over plenty of black pepper. Leave the kebabs to stand at room temperature for 2 hours.

Heat the grill to high and, if you have an open

wire rack, cover it with foil. Lay the kebabs on the hot rack and grill them for 10 to 15 minutes, turning them several times, until all the ingredients are cooked through.

Serve the kebabs on a bed of lettuce or salad leaves, garnished with radishes.

☆　　☆　　☆

Chef's tips:
☆ Accompany the mackerel with hot rice, either plain or cooked in stock with chopped

onions and a spice such as turmeric and/or paprika. Jacket or sauté potatoes are also suitable.
☆ An additional green salad may be needed besides the garnish.
☆ To freeze, cool completely and put a piece of cork onto the end of each kebab skewer for safety. Wrap each kebab individually in foil. To reheat, put the kebabs, still wrapped, into a preheated 400F/200C/gas 6 oven for 15 minutes, having removed the corks.
☆ To serve as a first course, halve all quantities and use small kebab skewers.

MACKEREL FILLETS WITH PIQUANT SAUCE

Serves: 4
Type of dish: Hot main course
Suitable for first course: yes, see below
Preparation time: 45 minutes
Waiting time: nil
Cooking time: 30 minutes
Preparation start: 1¼ hours before serving
Suitable for dinner parties: yes
Special equipment: large, heavy frying pan
Suitable for microwave cooking: no
Suitable for pressure cooking: no
Suitable for freezing: yes
Calorie content: high
Carbohydrate content: low
Fibre content: low
Protein content: high
Fat content: high

4 small to medium sized mackerel
2 oz (50 g) wholemeal flour
salt and pepper
1½ oz (40 g) butter
½ pint (275 ml) dry cider
2 tablespoons tomato purée
2 tablespoons grated horseradish
¼ teaspoon cayenne pepper

Fillet the mackerel (page 5). Put the flour onto a large, flat plate and add salt and pepper. Turn the mackerel fillets in the flour so that they become evenly coated. Leave them on a plate or work surface in a single layer until you are ready to fry them.

Melt 1 oz (25 g) of the butter in a frying pan on a medium heat. Put in as many of the mackerel fillets as will fit in a single layer, skin side down. Cook them until the first side is golden brown. Turn them over and brown the other side. Remove them to a serving dish and keep them warm. Add the rest of the butter. Put in the remaining mackerel fillets, cook them in the same way and arrange them on the serving dish with the others.

Pour the cider into the pan and bring it to the boil. Stir in the tomato purée, horseradish and cayenne pepper. Bring the mixture to the boil and cook it until it is reduced by about one third, stirring frequently. Pour the resulting sauce over the mackerel and serve as soon as possible.

☆   ☆   ☆

Chef's tips:

☆ Garnish the mackerel with sprigs of fresh herbs, such as parsley, fennel, chervil or coriander. Salad cress or attractive salad leaves such as those of battavia or endive can also be used.

☆ For horseradish, see page 13.

☆ Chili powder can be used instead of cayenne pepper.

☆ If no dry cider is available, a medium dry can be used but sweet ciders are not suitable.

☆ 3 fl oz (90 ml) olive oil or good quality sunflower oil can be used instead of butter.

☆ Serve with a green salad or with lightly-cooked green vegetables such as broccoli,

mange tout peas or green cabbage.

☆ Suggested potato accompaniments are sauté, or plainly-boiled new potatoes, tossed with parsley and butter.

☆ Lightly cooked plain pasta can also be served with this dish.

☆ To freeze, lay the fish in a plastic container with foil or greaseproof paper between the pieces. Freeze the sauce in a separate covered container. Store for up to two weeks. Thaw in the refrigerator and reheat the mackerel by frying it quickly in a little butter. Heat the sauce in a small saucepan.

☆ To serve as a first course, use small mackerel and serve one fillet per person; or use one medium mackerel and serve half a fillet, cut crosswise before cooking, per person. Halve all other ingredients.

SMOKED AND FRESH MACKEREL WITH HOT WATERCRESS SALAD

Serves: 4
Type of dish: Hot main course
Suitable for first course: yes, see below
Preparation time: 30 minutes
Cooking time: 30 minutes
Preparation start: 1 hour before serving
Suitable for dinner parties: yes
Special equipment: large, heavy frying pan
Suitable for microwave cooking: no
Suitable for pressure cooking: no
Suitable for freezing: mackerel only
Calorie content: high
Carbohydrate content: low
Fibre content: medium
Protein content: high
Fat content: high

2 medium-sized fresh mackerel
2 cold-smoked mackerel fillets (page 11)
2 oz (50 g) wholemeal flour
salt and pepper
2 bunches watercress
12 oz (350 g) firm tomatoes
1 large orange
2 tablespoons white wine vinegar
1 teaspoon Dijon mustard
4 tablespoons sunflower oil
1 garlic clove, finely chopped

Fillet the fresh mackerel (page 5) and cut each fillet in half crossways. Cut each smoked mackerel fillet in half crossways. Put the flour onto a large, flat plate and add salt and pepper. Turn the pieces of mackerel in the flour so that they become evenly coated.

Chop the watercress, removing the lower parts of the stems. Slice the tomatoes into rings. Cut the peel and pith from the orange. Cut the flesh into lengthways quarters and thinly slice each quarter. Mix together the vinegar and the mustard.

Heat the oil in a frying pan on a medium heat. Put in as many pieces of mackerel that the pan will take in a single layer, cut side down first, and brown them on both sides. Remove them and keep them warm. Cook any remaining pieces of mackerel in the same way and put them with the rest. Put the garlic into the pan and let it sizzle. Put the watercress, tomatoes and orange into the pan, and stir-fry them for 1 minute, or until they are just heated through but still re-

main crisp and fresh. Pour in the vinegar mixture and let it bubble. Remove the salad from the heat immediately. Divide it between four individual plates. Set the cooked mackerel fillets on top.

☆   ☆   ☆

Chef's tips:
☆ The mackerel fillets can be garnished with either small pieces of tomato or with a little extra salad cress, each raw. Serve with jacket potatoes or sauté potatoes.
☆ Any mild French-type mustard can replace the Dijon mustard. Use a smooth, rather than a grainy one, or use a smooth German mustard.
☆ Once the mackerel is cooked it can be kept warm for up to 30 minutes, but the salad must be served as soon as it comes off the heat.

STIR-FRIED MACKEREL WITH CUCUMBER AND TOMATOES

Serves: 4
Type of dish: Hot main course
Suitable for first course: yes, see below
Preparation time: 30 minutes
Waiting time: nil
Cooking time: 5 minutes
Preparation start: 35 minutes before serving
Suitable for dinner parties: yes
Special equipment: wok or heavy frying pan
Suitable for microwave cooking: no
Suitable for pressure cooking: no
Suitable for freezing: no
Calorie content: high
Carbohydrate content: low
Fibre content: low
Protein content: high
Fat content: high

4 medium mackerel
½ cucumber
8 oz (225 g) tomatoes
4 tablespoons olive oil
I garlic clove, finely chopped
I tablespoon chopped dill, or I teaspoon dried dill weed
I tablespoon chopped basil, or I teaspoon dried
I tablespoon white wine vinegar

Fillet the mackerel (page 5) and cut the fillets into strips about ½ inch (1.3 cm) wide. Halve the cucumber lengthways, without peeling, and thinly slice the halves. Chop the tomatoes.

Heat the oil in a large frying pan or wok on a high heat. Put in the mackerel strips and stir them over the heat for about 2 minutes, or until they are cooked through but not falling apart. Remove the mackerel pieces and keep them warm.

Put the cucumber and garlic into the pan and stir-fry them until they are just beginning to brown, about 3 minutes. Add the tomatoes and herbs and stir-fry them for 30 seconds so the tomatoes heat through but do not become soft. Add the vinegar and let it bubble. Carefully mix in the mackerel. Take the pan from the heat and serve immediately.

☆   ☆   ☆

Chef's tips:
☆ As this dish requires very little time to prepare or cook and because it is best served

immediately, ensure that any accompaniment is ready at the same time or just before. This may mean starting it before the mackerel.

☆ Make sure that the mackerel is only just cooked through. If it is over-cooked it may end up as a mush.

☆ Serve with boiled new potatoes tossed with butter and chopped fresh herbs such as parsley alone, parsley and chives or parsley and fennel; or with old potatoes, sliced in their skins, lightly boiled for 10 minutes and tossed with butter and similar herbs; or with tagliatelle tossed with grated Parmesan cheese, crushed garlic and butter.

☆ For a dish with a Chinese flavour, omit the tomatoes and herbs, stir-fry a little freshly grated ginger and six chopped spring onions with the cucumber and garlic and use 2 tablespoons of soy sauce instead of the wine vinegar.

MIDDLE EASTERN COLD MACKEREL

Serves: 4
Type of dish: Cold main course
Suitable for first course: yes, see below
Preparation time: 40 minutes
Cooking time: 35 minutes
Waiting time: 2 hours for cooling and chilling
Preparation start: 3½ hours before serving
Suitable for dinner parties: yes, and buffet parties
Special equipment: large, heavy frying pan or sauté pan, with lid
Suitable for microwave cooking: no
Suitable for pressure cooking: no
Suitable for freezing: yes
Calorie content: high
Carbohydrate content: low
Fibre content: low
Protein content: high
Fat content: high

4 small - medium mackerel
1½ oz (40 g) flour
salt and freshly-ground black pepper
2 medium onions
2 green peppers
2 garlic cloves
3 fl oz (90 ml) olive oil
one 14 oz (400 g) tin chopped tomatoes in juice
¼ pint (150 ml) tomato juice
salt and freshly-ground black pepper
2 tablespoons chopped parsley
2 oz (50 g) black olives

Fillet the mackerel and cut each fillet in half crossways. Put the flour onto a plate and season it with the salt and pepper. Coat the pieces of mackerel in the seasoned flour.

Thinly slice the onions. Core and seed the peppers and cut them into thin strips. Crush the garlic.

Heat 4 tablespoons of the oil in a large, heavy frying pan on a medium heat. Put in the pieces of mackerel and fry them so they brown on both sides but do not cook completely through. Remove them.

Put the remaining oil into the pan and lower the heat. Put in the onion and fry it for about 5 minutes so it begins to soften. Put in the peppers and continue to fry, stirring frequently, for a further 5 minutes. Stir in the crushed garlic and then add the tomatoes and the tomato juice. Season, and simmer everything for 5 minutes. Put the mackerel fillets back into the pan and spoon a little of the liquid over it. Cover and

simmer for 5 minutes, or until the mackerel is cooked through but not breaking up.

Lift out the pieces of mackerel and arrange them in a shallow dish. Add the olives to the pan and then boil the liquid, uncovered, until it has reduced by about half and has thickened.

Pour all the contents of the pan over the mackerel. Cool the mackerel to room temperature and then chill it in the refrigerator for about 30 minutes before serving.

☆   ☆   ☆

Chef's tips:
☆ Garnish with sprigs of parsley, fennel or fresh coriander if wished.
☆ Serve with a salad of rice, bulgar wheat or pasta.
☆ To freeze, put the mackerel from the pan into a rigid plastic container. Cool sauce before pouring it over the mackerel. Cover and store for up to three weeks. Thaw in the refrigerator and transfer carefully to a serving dish, taking care not to break up the mackerel.

MACKEREL AND SALAMI SALAD

Serves: 4
Type of dish: Cold main course
Suitable for first course: yes, see below
1st preparation time: 30 minutes
Cooking time: 5 minutes
Waiting time: 24 hours
Preparation start: 24 hours before serving
Suitable for dinner parties: yes
Special equipment: frying pan
Suitable for microwave cooking: yes
Suitable for pressure cooking: no
Suitable for freezing: no
Calorie content: high
Carbohydrate content: low
Fibre content: low
Protein content: high
Fat content: high

4 small - medium mackerel
4 tablespoons olive oil
juice 1 lemon
2 oz (50 g) Italian salami, in thin slices
2 tablespoons chopped fresh coriander
1 tablespoon chopped thyme
freshly-ground black pepper
1 escarole, battavia or frisée lettuce
8 radishes
6 celery sticks

Fillet the mackerel (page 5). Cut the fillets into pieces about ¾ by ½ inch (2 by 1.5 cm).

Heat the oil in a frying pan on a medium heat. Put in the pieces of mackerel and toss them in the oil until they are just cooked through but still firm and unbrowned. Take the pan from the heat and transfer the mackerel and oil to a bowl. Pour in the lemon juice and gently fold it into the oil, taking care not to break up the mackerel. Leave the mackerel until it is quite cold, then cover the bowl and leave the mackerel at room temperature for 24 hours.

Cut the slices of salami into quarters. Fold the salami and herbs into the mackerel and season with the pepper.

Separate the leaves of the lettuce. Thinly slice the radishes. Cut the celery sticks into very thin crossways slices. Arrange a bed of lettuce leaves on each of four serving plates. Put a portion of the mackerel salad in the centre. Put slices of radish on the lettuce leaves and portions of the sliced celery in between.

Chef's tips:

☆ The salad garnish may be varied according to availability. For example, watercress or another type of lettuce may be used as a base.

☆ If fresh coriander is unavailable, use parsley.

☆ Serve with warm, crusty bread or rolls.

☆ To serve as a first course, halve the amounts of mackerel, keep the amounts of salami the same and have enough salad to taste. Keep the bread rolls as an accompaniment, or serve toast instead.

MACKEREL BAKED IN FOIL

Serves: 4
Type of dish: hot main course (two)
Suitable for first course: no
Preparation time: 30 minutes
Waiting time: 1 hour for *Mackerel with Nutmeg*
Cooking time: 20 minutes
Preparation start: *Mackerel with Herbs*, 1 hour before serving; *Mackerel with Nutmeg*, 2 hours before serving
Suitable for dinner parties: yes
Special equipment: foil, baking sheet
Suitable for microwave cooking: yes, in dish, not in foil
Suitable for pressure cooking: no
Suitable for freezing: no
Calorie content: high
Carbohydrate content: low
Fibre content: low
Protein content: high
Fat content: high

4 small - medium mackerel
for Mackerel filled with Herbs:
3 oz (75 g) butter
juice ½ lemon
2 shallots or button onions, or 1 small onion
2 tablespoons chopped parsley
1 tablespoon chopped thyme, or 1 teaspoon dried
1 tablespoon grated preserved horseradish
freshly-ground black pepper
1 lemon, cut into wedges
for Mackerel with Nutmeg:
4 tablespoons olive oil
juice ½ lemon
¼ nutmeg, freshly grated, or ½ teaspoon ground nutmeg
freshly-ground black pepper
4 tablespoons chopped parsley
1 lemon, cut into wedges

Clean the mackerel. Cut off the fins and tails but leave the heads on. Rinse the fish under running water and dry them with paper towels.

For the *Mackerel filled with Herbs,* cream the butter and gradually beat in the lemon juice. Beat in the shallots, herbs and horseradish and season with the pepper. Put an equal amount of the mixture into the cavity of each fish.

For the *Mackerel with Nutmeg,* beat together the oil, lemon juice, nutmeg and pepper. Put the mackerel into a flat dish and brush them inside and out with the mixture. Pour any remaining mixture over them and leave them for 1 hour at

room temperature. Just before cooking, put 1 tablespoon parsley and one lemon wedge inside each fish.

Heat the oven to 375F/190C/gas 5. Cut four squares of aluminium foil large enough to give about 6 inches (15 cm) overlap on the sides of the mackerel and 4 inches (10 cm) at each end. Bring the sides of the foil together and seal the edges by folding them inwards. Fold the ends upwards a couple of times to prevent any juices from leaking out.

Lay the parcels on a baking sheet and put them into the oven for 20 minutes.

Unwrap the parcels and turn the mackerel onto individual plates. Serve garnished with the lemon wedges.

☆　　☆　　☆

Chef's tips:
☆ Parsley sprigs, watercress or salad cress can be used for additional garnish.
☆ Serve with sauté potatoes, jacket potatoes or potatoes that have been cut into slices and roasted in a mixture of oil and butter.
☆ Serve with a mixed or green salad or lightly cooked green vegetables.
☆ For horseradish, see glossary, page 12.

BAKED ROLLED MACKEREL WITH HERB SAUCE

Serves: 4
Type of dish: Hot main course
Suitable for first course: no
1st preparation time: 45 minutes
Waiting time: nil
Cooking time: 30 minutes
2nd preparation time: 20 minutes (concurrent with cooking time)
Preparation start: 1¼ hours before serving
Suitable for dinner parties: yes
Special equipment: flat, oven-proof dish
Suitable for microwave cooking: yes
Suitable for pressure cooking: not sauce
Suitable for freezing: no
Calorie content: high
Carbohydrate content: low
Fibre content: low
Protein content: high
Fat content: high

4 medium sized mackerel
½ teaspoon ground mace
2 tablespoons chopped parsley
2 tablespoons chopped fennel
1 small onion
3 fl oz (90 ml) water
2 tablespoons malt vinegar
sauce:
2 egg yolks
1 tablespoon chopped parsley
1 tablespoon chopped fennel
2 tablespoons malt vinegar
4 oz (125 g) unsalted butter, in small pieces
for serving:
1 tablespoon each of chopped mixed parsley and fennel

Heat the oven to 400F/200C/gas 6.

Make each fish into one large fillet, joined down the back but with the backbone removed (page 5). Remove the tails.

Lay the fillets flat and sprinkle each one with mace and herbs. Roll up the fillets, starting at the tail end. Secure them by tying them at each end with fine cotton string (not too tightly or the string may slice into the fillets as they cook).

Thinly slice the onion and scatter it in the base of a flat, ovenproof dish. Set the mackerel rolls on top and pour in the water and vinegar. Cover the dish with foil and put it into the oven for 20 minutes.

Make the *sauce* while the mackerel are cooking. Put the egg yolks, herbs and vinegar into a small saucepan and stir them with a wooden spoon on a very low heat until the mixture begins to thicken. Do not let it boil or it will curdle. Quickly stir in the butter. As soon as it has melted and is well mixed into the egg mixture, remove the pan from the heat. Spoon portions of the sauce onto each of four individual plates.

Take the mackerel from the oven, cut off the string and set the fillets on top of the pools of sauce. Scatter a sprinkling of herbs over the top.

☆ ☆ ☆

Chef's tips:

☆ If no fennel is available use thyme, lemon thyme or marjoram.

☆ If parsley is the only fresh herb available you can substitute the second fresh herb with ½ teaspoon dried thyme or marjoram, sprinkling it over the fish very lightly. For garnishing, use parsley only.

☆ Serve with a selection of lightly cooked vegetables such as courgettes, carrots, peas or mange tout peas, cauliflower or green beans.

☆ The potatoes should be new potatoes, plainly boiled in their skins or sauté potatoes.

☆ Should you find the heat under your saucepan too fierce, use a double saucepan which consists of a small pan resting on another pan filled with water, or use a basin standing in a saucepan of water.

SOUSED MACKEREL WITH GOOSEBERRY SAUCE

Serves: 4
Type of dish: Cold main course
Suitable for first course: yes, see below
1st preparation time: 45 minutes
Cooking time: 30 minutes
Waiting time: 1 - 1½ hours to cool
2nd preparation time: 20 minutes
Preparation start: 2¼ hours before serving
Suitable for dinner parties: yes
Special equipment: flat, oven-proof dish
Suitable for microwave cooking: yes
Suitable for pressure cooking: yes
Suitable for freezing: no
Calorie content: high
Carbohydrate content: low
Fibre content: low
Protein content: high
Fat content: high

4 small mackerel
oil for greasing
¼ nutmeg, grated, or ¼ teaspoon ground nutmeg
two 2 inch (5 cm) cinnamon sticks
1 medium onion
8 oz (225 g) gooseberries
4 tablespoons dry cider
2 teaspoons sugar

Heat the oven to 350F/180C/gas 4. Lightly oil a flat, ovenproof dish that will take the mackerel fillets in a single layer.

Fillet the mackerel (page 5) and lay the fillets, skin-side down, in the dish. Grate or sprinkle over the nutmeg and put a piece of cinnamon at either side of the dish. Thinly slice the onion and scatter it over the mackerel. Top and tail and chop the gooseberries and strew them on top of the onion. Pour in the cider. Sprinkle the sugar around the mackerel. Cover the dish with foil and put it into the oven for 30 minutes.

Leave the mackerel, still covered, at room temperature until it is quite cold.

Gently brush all the pieces of onion and gooseberry from the mackerel and lay the cold cooked fillets on a serving dish.

Remove the cinnamon sticks from the dish and rub the remaining contents through a sieve to make a purée. Stir the purée so it becomes a smooth, creamy-textured sauce. Spoon the sauce over the mackerel.

☆　　☆　　☆

Chef's tips:
☆ Garnish with fennel or parsley sprigs and/or with sliced radishes.
☆ For added effect, lay the mackerel on a bed of fresh vine leaves or lemon balm leaves.
☆ Serve with a potato or rice salad and a selection of vegetable salads, but keep the flavours quite mild so the subtle flavour of the gooseberries is not lost. Alternatively, serve hot jacket or plainly boiled potatoes.
☆ To serve as a first course, use two small mackerel and keep the rest of the ingredients as above.

MARINATED MACKEREL BRAISED WITH CELERY

Serves: 4
Type of dish: Hot main course
Suitable for first course: no
Preparation time: 45 minutes
Waiting time: 2 hours
Cooking time: 45 minutes
Preparation start: 3½ hours before serving
Suitable for dinner parties: yes
Special equipment: wide based casserole
Suitable for microwave cooking: yes
Suitable for pressure cooking: yes
Suitable for freezing: yes
Calorie content: high
Carbohydrate content: low
Fibre content: low
Protein content: high
Fat content: high

4 small to medium mackerel
freshly-ground black pepper
1 small onion
8 fl oz (225 ml) dry white wine or cider
1 tablespoon preserved grated horseradish
2 teaspoons smooth, mild French or German mustard
1 tablespoon chopped thyme, or 1 teaspoon dried
1 tablespoon chopped parsley
1 head celery
1 oz (25 g) butter
2 tablespoons chopped parsley

Fillet the mackerel (page 5), cut the fillets in half crossways and season them with the pepper. Finely chop the onion. Mix together the wine, horseradish and mustard. Put the mackerel fillets into a large, flat dish. Pour in the wine mixture.

Scatter the onion and herbs over the top. Cover the mackerel and let it stand for 2 hours at room temperature.

Heat the oven to 350F/180C/gas 4. Lift out the mackerel and brush off as much of the marinade as possible. Strain the marinade, reserving both the liquid and solid parts. Cut the celery into 1 inch (2.5 cm) pieces.

Melt the butter in a wide-based casserole on a low heat. Stir in the celery plus the contents of the sieve. Cover them and leave them on the low heat for 7 minutes. Put the mackerel fillets on top of the celery. Pour in the liquid part of the

marinade and bring it to the boil. Cover the casserole again and put it into the oven for 30 minutes.

Serve the mackerel on a bed of celery with the cooking liquids poured over them and a little chopped parsley scattered over the top.

☆   ☆   ☆

Chef's tips:
☆ Serve with a selection of lightly cooked veg-

etables of contrasting colours plus plainly boiled potatoes or jacket potatoes.

☆ For horseradish, see glossary, page 12.

☆ Cooking the celery in the marinade that was used for the mackerel blends all the flavours together. Any hotness in the horseradish disappears, leaving a good, savoury flavour.

☆ Cooking the celery for this amount of time in the oven leaves it fairly crisp. Should you wish it to be softer, cook the celery in the covered casserole in the oven for 15 minutes before you put the mackerel on top and continue cooking for a further 30 minutes.

☆ To freeze, cool the contents of the casserole and transfer them to a plastic container, taking care not to break up the mackerel. Cover and store for up to two weeks. Thaw very slightly so the mackerel and vegetables can be transferred again to the casserole. Reheat by putting into a preheated 200C/400F/gas 6 oven for 20 minutes.

FINNISH MACKEREL HOTPOT

Serves: 4
Type of dish: Hot main course
Suitable for first course: no
Preparation time: 45 minutes
Waiting time: nil
Cooking time: 30 minutes
Preparation start: 1¼ hours before serving
Suitable for dinner parties: no
Special equipment: large, heavy saucepan with
 lid
Suitable for microwave cooking: yes
Suitable for pressure cooking: yes
Suitable for freezing: yes
Calorie content: high
Carbohydrate content: medium
Fibre content: medium
Protein content: high
Fat content: medium

4 medium mackerel
2 lb (900 g) potatoes
4 allspice berries, crushed
½ teaspoon salt
freshly-ground black pepper
grated rind ½ lemon
1 tablespoon egg white
1 teaspoon cornflour
¼ pint (150 ml) natural yoghurt
4 tablespoons chopped parsley

Fillet the mackerel (page 5) and cut them into 1 inch (2.5 cm) square pieces. Scrub the potatoes but do not peel them and cut them into ½ inch (1.3 cm) dice.

Put the potatoes into a saucepan with the allspice, salt, plenty of pepper, the lemon rind and 1 pint (550 ml) water. Bring them to the boil and simmer them for 15 - 20 minutes, or until they are just cooked through. Add the mackerel and simmer for a further 5 minutes so it is cooked through but not falling apart.

While the potatoes are cooking, put the egg white and cornflour into a small saucepan and stir in the yoghurt. Set them on a medium heat and bring them to the boil, stirring. Simmer, still stirring, for about 5 minutes, or until the mixture is thick. When the mackerel is cooked, stir the yogurt mixture into the pan and reheat the rest of the contents if necessary.

Turn everything onto a serving dish or onto individual plates, and scatter the parsley over the top.

Chef's tips:

☆ Serve with a green salad or with lightly cooked green vegetables. No other accompaniment is necessary.

☆ To freeze, do not add the yoghurt mixture. Cool the potatoes and mackerel completely. Put them into a plastic container and cover.

Store for up to two weeks. Thaw in the refrigerator and reheat gently in a saucepan before adding the yoghurt as above.

☆ Treating yoghurt this way is called stabilizing yoghurt. It is done to prevent the yoghurt from curdling or separating when it is stirred into hot liquid. You can make up double quantities and store it in the refrigerator in a covered container for up to one week.

☆ Allspice, sometimes called Jamaican pepper, is a mild, aromatic spice. Crushed berries always have more flavour than the ground variety, although ground allspice may be used if whole berries are unavailable. To crush the berries, use a small pestle and mortar.

☆ As an alternative, use 2 teaspoons paprika plus ¼ teaspoon cayenne pepper instead of the allspice and black pepper.

MARINATED MACKEREL PATE

Serves: 4 as main course, 8 as first course
Type of dish: Cold main or first course
Suitable for first course: yes
1st preparation time: 30 minutes
1st waiting time: 4 hours
Cooking time: 7 minutes
2nd waiting time: 1½ hours for cooling
Preparation start: 6 hours before serving
Suitable for dinner parties: yes, as first course
Special equipment: Large, shallow dish; grill; dish for finished paté
Suitable for microwave cooking: yes
Suitable for pressure cooking: no
Suitable for freezing: yes
Calorie content: high
Carbohydrate content: low
Fibre content: low
Protein content: high
Fat content: high

1 small onion
1 garlic clove
grated rind and juice ½ lemon
2 tablespoons olive oil
6 thyme sprigs, or 1 teaspoon dried thyme
freshly-ground black pepper
2 medium mackerel
8 oz (225 g) hot-smoked mackerel fillet (page 11)
1 tablespoon grated horseradish
1 tablespoon chopped capers

Finely chop the onion and garlic. Put them into a large, flat dish. Add the lemon rind and mix in the oil. Add the thyme sprigs or sprinkle in the dried thyme, and season with the pepper.

Fillet the fresh mackerel. Turn these fillets and the smoked mackerel fillets in the marinade and leave them cut side down. Cover the dish with foil or cling film and leave the mackerel for 4 hours at room temperature.

To cook, heat the grill on a high heat and, if you have an open, wire rack, cover it with foil. Without brushing the pieces of marinade from them (apart from the thyme sprigs), lay the mackerel fillets, skin side down, on the hot grill rack or foil. Cook them until the smoked fillets are heated through and the fresh fillets are cooked through and beginning to turn golden, about 7 minutes. There is no need to turn them.

Remove the fillets to a plate, turn them over and scrape off the skins. Put the flesh into a bowl and beat it to a purée with a wooden spoon or large wooden pestle. Work in the capers and horseradish. Pack the mixture into an oiled dish or mould. Cover it and chill it for about 1½ hours, or until it is firm.

To serve, turn the paté from the mould and cut it into slices.

☆   ☆   ☆

Chef's tips:

☆ If you are serving the paté as a main course, serve it with a selection of salads.

☆ Serve a potato or rice salad or jacket potatoes.

☆ When serving the paté as a first course, cut smaller portions and garnish them with salad leaves and a twist of lemon or orange.

☆ To accompany a first course, have thin slices of hot toast or heated bread rolls or French bread.

☆ For horseradish, see glossary, page 12.

☆ To freeze, turn the paté out of the mould, wrap it in clingfilm and then put it into a polythene bag. Seal the top. Store for up to two weeks.

SMOKED MACKEREL PASTIES

Serves: 4
Type of dish: Hot or cold main course
Suitable for first course: no
Preparation time: 45 minutes
Waiting time: nil
Cooking time: 20 minutes
Preparation start: 1 hour 5 minutes before serving hot (if serving cold, allow cooling time)
Suitable for dinner parties: no
Special equipment: baking sheet; oven
Suitable for microwave cooking: no
Suitable for pressure cooking: no
Suitable for freezing: yes
Calorie content: high
Carbohydrate content: medium
Fibre content: medium
Protein content: high
Fat content: high

pastry:		
8 oz (225 g) wholemeal flour		
4 oz (125 g) butter or dripping		
pinch salt		
cold water to mix		
1 egg, beaten, for glaze		
filling:		
12 oz (350 g) hot-smoked mackerel fillets (page 11)		
4 medium-sized firm tomatoes		
3 tablespoons chopped fennel		

Heat the oven to 400F/200C/gas 6. Make the *pastry*. Put the flour into a mixing bowl with the salt. Add the butter, in small pieces, and rub it into the flour. Mix to a dough with the cold water and leave it in a cool place for 15 minutes.

Skin the mackerel fillets, remove any bones and flake the flesh. Halve the tomatoes and thinly slice each half crossways. Mix the tomatoes and fennel into the mackerel.

Divide the pastry into four equal pieces and roll each piece into a round. Lay the rounds on floured baking sheets. Put one quarter of the mackerel mixture over half of each round of pastry. Fold the other side of the pastry over the top and seal the edges. Brush the pasties with the beaten egg and bake them for 20 minutes or until they are golden brown.

Either serve the pasties hot, while the insides are still bubbling, or leave them to get completely cold.

☆　　☆　　☆

Chef's tips:

☆ Whether the pasties are being served for a hot or a cold meal, the best accompaniment is a selection of salads.

☆ Potato or rice salads are suitable and so are jacket potatoes.

☆ The pasties make an ideal snack for a picnic or lunch box.

☆ White flour or a half-and-half mixture may be used instead of wholemeal if wished. In this case, the fibre content of the recipe will be lowered.

☆ If fennel is not available, use parsley plus 1 teaspoon paprika.

SMOKED MACKEREL WITH RICE AND TOMATOES

Serves: 4
Type of dish: Hot main course
Suitable for first course: no
Preparation time: 20 minutes
Waiting time: nil
1st cooking time: 40 minutes (for rice)
2nd cooking time: 10 minutes (for dish)
Preparation start: 1¼ hours before serving
Suitable for dinner parties: no
Special equipment: saucepan; frying pan
Suitable for microwave cooking: rice only
Suitable for pressure cooking: rice only
Suitable for freezing: yes
Calorie content: high
Carbohydrate content: high
Fibre content: high
Protein content: high
Fat content: medium

8 oz (225 g) long grain brown rice
½ teaspoon salt
1 lb (450 g) hot-smoked mackerel fillets (page 11)
1 lb (450 g) tomatoes
1 large onion
1 oz (25 g) butter or 3 tablespoons olive or sunflower oil
1 garlic clove, finely chopped
2 tablespoons chopped fresh basil or 2 teaspoons dried
3 tablespoons cider vinegar

Put the rice into a saucepan with the salt and 1 pint (550 ml) cold water. Bring it to the boil. Cover and simmer for 40 minutes or until the rice is tender and all the water has been absorbed.

While the rice is cooking, skin and flake the mackerel. Put the tomatoes into a bowl, and pour boiling water over them. Leave them for 2 minutes, drain them and peel away the skins. They should slip off quite easily. Slice the tomatoes crossways into rings. Thinly slice the onion.

Melt the butter or heat the oil in a large frying pan on a low heat. Put in the onion and garlic and cook them until they are soft, stirring occasionally. If you are using dried basil, add it to the pan just before the onions are done.

Raise the heat to the highest temperature and quickly mix in the tomatoes, mackerel and rice. Add the fresh basil at this point. Keep stirring the contents of the pan with a fork so that they heat through evenly. This will take about 2 minutes. The tomatoes should stay firm. Add the vinegar and mix it in well.

Serve either from one large dish or on individual plates.

Chef's tips:

☆ Garnish with chopped fresh parsley or with parsley sprigs, if wished.

☆ Serve with a selection of vegetables such as broccoli, green beans, baby corn or sweetcorn kernels, braised celery, peas or mange tout peas.

☆ Alternatively, serve with a green salad.

☆ Additional vegetables can be added to the rice mixture such as 4 - 6 oz (125 - 175 g) cooked peas and/or sweetcorn, or 4 - 6 celery sticks that have been chopped and fried gently with the onions and garlic.

☆ To freeze, cool the finished dish completely and pack it into a plastic container. Cover and store for up to two weeks. Thaw in the refrigerator and reheat by tossing in melted butter or a little olive or sunflower oil in a frying pan or saucepan on a medium heat.

SMOKED MACKEREL
SALMAGUNDY

Serves: 4
Type of dish: Cold main course
Suitable for first course: yes, see below
Preparation time: 45 minutes
Waiting time: nil
Cooking time: nil
Preparation start: 45 minutes before serving
Suitable for dinner parties: lunch party
Special equipment: electric beater for mayonnaise, optional
Suitable for microwave cooking: no
Suitable for pressure cooking: no
Suitable for freezing: no
Calorie content: medium
Carbohydrate content: low
Fibre content: medium
Protein content: high
Fat content: medium

dressing:
1 egg yolk
freshly-ground black pepper
½ teaspoon mustard powder
4 tablespoons olive or sunflower oil
¼ pint (150 ml) natural yoghurt
salad:
1 medium-sized crisp green lettuce, or 3 small Little Gem lettuces
2 oz (50 g) watercress
1 medium-sized cooking apple
8 oz (225 g) cooked beetroot
2 tablespoons preserved grated horseradish
1 teaspoon dill seeds
12 oz (350 g) hot-smoked mackerel fillets (page 11)
4 hard-boiled eggs

For the dressing, put the egg yolk into a bowl with the pepper and mustard powder. Beat together, either with a wooden spoon or with an electric beater. Beat in the oil, drop by drop, and then gradually beat in the yoghurt to make a smooth, creamy mayonnaise.

Chop the lettuce and watercress. Mix them together and divide them between four fairly large bowls. Spoon half the dressing over the top.

Skin and flake the mackerel fillets. Divide the mackerel between the four bowls, putting it into the centre.

Quarter and core the apple and cut it into ¼ inch (6 mm) dice. Cut the beetroot into pieces

the same size. Mix the apple and beetroot with the remaining mayonnaise and the horseradish and dill. Arrange them around the mackerel.

Cut the hard boiled eggs into lengthways quarters and arrange them on top of the salads.

☆ ☆ ☆

Chef's tips:
☆ A salmagundy was an elaborate salad dish popular in the eighteenth century. It consisted of a base of fresh, leafy cresses and lettuce, topped with pieces of meat and game and garnished with hard boiled eggs and beetroot.

☆ Serve with warm white rolls or French bread or with thick chunks of mixed grain or wholemeal bread.

☆ To make the meal a more substantial one, the salad may be preceded by a thick soup.

☆ To serve as a first course, use 4 oz (125 g) smoked mackerel fillet and halve the rest of the ingredients.

☆ For horseradish, see page 13.

SMOKED MACKEREL AND PEPPER TART

Serves: 4
Type of dish: Hot or cold main course
Suitable for first course: yes, see below
Preparation time: 45 minutes
Waiting time: nil
Cooking time: 20 minutes
Preparation start: 1hr 5mins before serving
Suitable for dinner parties: buffet parties
Special equipment: 8 inch (20 cm) diameter tart tin
Suitable for microwave cooking: yes
Suitable for pressure cooking: no
Suitable for freezing: yes
Calorie content: high
Carbohydrate content: medium
Fibre content: medium
Protein content: high
Fat content: high

pastry:
6 oz (175 g) wholemeal flour
2 teaspoons paprika
pinch salt
3 oz (75 g) butter
cold water to mix

filling:
8 oz (225 g) hot-smoked mackerel fillets (page 11)
2 medium tomatoes
1 red pepper
1 green pepper
1 medium onion
1 oz (25 g) butter
3 eggs
¼ teaspoon cayenne pepper
5 fl oz (150 ml) milk

Heat the oven to 200C/400F/gas 6. For the pastry, put the flour into a mixing bowl with the paprika and salt. Add the butter, in small pieces, and rub it into the flour. Mix to a dough with cold water. Form the pastry into a ball and leave it in a cool place while you prepare the rest of the ingredients.

Skin and flake the mackerel. Thinly slice the tomatoes into crossways rounds.

Core and seed the peppers and cut them into thin, 1 inch (2.5 cm) strips. Thinly slice the onion. Melt the butter in a frying pan on a low heat. Put in the onion and strips of red and green pepper and cook gently until the onion is soft, stirring frequently. Tip the onion and peppers onto a plate to cool.

Roll out the pastry and use it to line an 8 inch (20 cm) diameter tart tin. Set the tin on a baking tray. Put in the onion and peppers in an even layer. Put in the flaked mackerel.

Beat the eggs together, adding the cayenne pepper. Gradually beat in the milk. Pour the egg and milk mixture into the tart tin. Decorate the top of the tart with the tomato rings.

Bake the tart for 20 minutes or until the top of the egg mixture is set and is golden brown on top.

Serve hot or cold.

Garnish with thinly-cut onion rings or rings of red and green pepper, or with parsley sprigs.

☆   ☆   ☆

Chef's tips:

☆ If the tart is to be served hot, jacket potatoes, sauté potatoes or French fries make good accompaniments, plus a green vegetable such as peas, green beans or broccoli.

☆ A green salad is the best accompaniment to a cold tart, plus any of the above potatoes or a potato salad.

☆ The wholemeal flour in the pastry can be replaced by white flour or with a half-and-half mixture of flours. In this case the fibre content of the recipe will be lowered.

☆ To freeze, remove the tart from the tin. Wrap it in clingfilm or secure it in a sealed polythene bag. Freeze it on a flat tray to keep it in shape. Store for up to two weeks. Alternatively, the tart may be cut into wedges which should then be individually wrapped before freezing flat and storing together in a polythene bag. This makes convenient lunch-box or picnic fare.

☆ To serve as a first course, make as above and cut into small wedges. Garnish with small pieces of lettuce.

SMOKED MACKEREL KOULIBIAC

Serves: 6
Type of dish: Cold main course
Suitable for first course: no
Preparation time: 2 hours
First waiting time: 1 hour 20 minutes, partly concurrent with preparation time
Cooking time: 30 minutes
Second waiting time: 1½ hours for cooling
Preparation start: 4½ hours before serving
Suitable for dinner parties: buffet parties
Special equipment: baking sheet, oven
Suitable for microwave cooking: no
Suitable for pressure cooking: no
Suitable for freezing: yes
Calorie content: high
Carbohydrate content: high
Fibre content: high
Protein content: medium
Fat content: medium

yeast pastry:
6 fl oz (175 g) milk, warmed
1 oz (25 g) fresh yeast or ½ oz (15 g) dried
1 teaspoon sugar (for dried yeast only)
1 lb (450 g) wholemeal flour
1 teaspoon salt
3 eggs, two beaten together, one separately
2 oz (50 g) butter, softened
filling:
4 oz (125 g) long grain brown rice, cooked and drained
8 fl oz (225 ml) vegetable stock pinch salt
8 oz (225 g) hot smoked mackerel fillet
4 oz (125 g) button mushrooms
2 oz (50 g) butter
1 medium onion, thinly sliced
6 eggs, hard boiled
2 tablespoons plain flour
½ pint (275 ml) vegetable stock
1 teaspoon mustard powder
1 tablespoon Dijon mustard
1 oz (25 g) parsley, chopped

Put the milk into a bowl and sprinkle in the yeast. Add the sugar if you are using dried yeast. Leave the yeast in a warm place for 10 minutes.

Put the flour and salt into a bowl. Make a well in the centre and put in the yeast mixture, the two beaten eggs, and the butter. Mix everything to a dough. Turn it onto a floured work surface and knead it until it is smooth. Return it to the bowl, cover it with a clean cloth and leave it in a warm place for one hour, or until it has doubled in size.

Skin and flake the mackerel fillets. Thinly slice the mushrooms. Melt 1 oz (25 g) of the butter in a frying pan on a low heat. Put in the onion and soften it. Raise the heat, put in the mushrooms and cook them, stirring, for 2 minutes. Remove them from the heat. Peel and slice the eggs.

For the sauce, put the stock into a saucepan with the remaining butter, flour and mustard powder. Set them on a medium heat and stir until the mixture boils and thickens. Take the pan from the heat and stir in the Dijon mustard and parsley.

Heat the oven to 400F / 200C / gas 6. Knead the dough again and divide it into two pieces, one slightly bigger than the other. Roll the smaller piece into a large rectangle, about 10 by 14 inches (25 by 35 cm) and lay it on a baking sheet.

Spread half the rice over it, leaving a gap of about 1½ inches (4 cm) round the edges. Put on half the mackerel, half the eggs, half the mushrooms and half the sauce. Repeat the layers again. Roll out the remaining pastry so it is about 2 inches (5 cm) longer and wider than the first piece. Cover the filling with this piece of pastry and seal the edges. Brush the top of the pastry with the one beaten egg.

Leave the koulibiac in a warm place for 20 minutes. Bake it for 30 minutes, or until it is golden brown. Cool it on a wire rack.

☆   ☆   ☆

Chef's tips:
☆ The whole koulibiac may be garnished with parsley sprigs, if wished. Serve cut into slices.
☆ The koulibiac comes from Russia and often contains salmon or some other type of oily fish. The outer casing is like very light bread in texture.
☆ A koulibiac is best served cold at parties and for special occasions.
☆ A selection of salads is the best accompaniment.
☆ To freeze, cool completely and wrap in foil or clingfilm. Freeze flat on a tray. Store for up to one month. Thaw in the refrigerator and then bring to room temperature before serving.